The Screech Owl

Issue 1 - January 2014

£4

ISBN 978-0-9561605-1-5
ISSN 2051-5529
© Resurgant Press (2014)

The Screech Owl
Issue 1 - January 2014

Published by Resurgant Press (2014)

© Resurgant Press (2014)

All work is © of their respective authors

All rights for the work inside belong to their respective authors.

The Screech Owl © 2014 Resurgant Press. All rights reserved.

ISBN 978-0-9561605-1-5

Cover artwork © Annette Haines (2014)

The Screech Owl - The Voice of Lilith

"Her castles shall be overgrown with thorns, her fortresses with thistles and briers. She shall become an abode for jackals and a haunt for ostriches"
- *Isaiah 34:13*

Welcome to the first issue of *The Screech Owl*. Hopefully she will be the first of many.

We are the voice of Lilith, a site (www.thescreechowl.com) and bi-annual magazine devoted to the best contemporary poetry, prose, short stories and articles.

Our goal is to give voice to both published and new writers, for voices can be lost or forgotten, emotions ignored for the sake of vanity or greed and the blood of the fallen trampled into the gutter's wash, poetry is the written embodiment of the human spirit and fields this pain, this love with equal ferocity.
Good literature shows the variety and endurance that Mankind can share and we at *The Screech Owl* wish to offer some of the best, new voices that embody such characteristics that we find are the better aspects in the turbulent nature of humanity.

I would like to take this opportunity of giving my grateful thanks for their invaluable guidance and assistance in the creation of our pet *Owl* to the following; Ben Fisher for his championing of my work & always accurate advice, Christopher James Heyworth for his knowledge and wise guidance, Annette Haines for her spark of divine creation that made *The Screech Owl* come to life and finally to the late Geoff Stevens of *Purple Patch*, a mentor and editor who can never be replaced.

Thank you, the reader, for your interest and support in us, we hope to repay your intrigued eyes with some quality work.

Thanks also to all the writers included here, we look forward to working with you all in the future.

Keep an eye on the skies for issue two of *The Screech Owl*, due summer 2014. Please visit our website for up to date work and information.

Also, 'like' our Facebook page and follow us on Twitter @TheScreechOwl1 for finger tip fresh facts.

See you in the sunshine.

Grant Tarbard
Editor

Submissions

Email: editors@thescreechowl.com

Any other comments please use the contacts **page on the website or email**
thescreechowl@hotmail.com

Please send all submissions, with a short bio, in the body of an email.
No more than 5 poems, 2 reviews/articles of up to 2 pages each or 1 piece of prose up to 1,000 words please.

We are not adherent followers of any styles or trends, your verse can be free or structured, it doesn't matter. We look for thoughtful, intelligent verse and work.

If you have to use snail mail then please include a S. A. E. Thank you.

Address:
The Screech Owl, 8 Chancel Close, Laindon, Basildon, Essex SS15 5FF

Contents

Editor's Note

Submissions

The Apple Tree (Poetry & Prose)-

'Sleep' - Martin Slidel

'Folly' - David Seddon

'GroBe Geister (Large Ghosts)' - Neil Ellman

'Vampyre' - Grant Tarbard

'Caff' - Ben Fisher

'Anais, Anais' - Sarah Farrant

'David Cameron on Scottish Independence' - Rob A. Mackenzie

'Chemistry' - Jonathan Beale

'Shirty Boat' - Ira Lightman

'Waiting for Wrecks' - C.J. Heyworth

'Street maps for lost souls' - John Dorsey

'Loss' Darrell Croan

'Insomnia II' - Klaus J. Gerken

'Incident on Fifty-second Street' - Joe Green

'I Collect Cities, Do You?' - Philip Burton

'Golden Globe' - Annette Haines

'Yo! Sushi' - Andrew F. Giles

'The Last Man on Lookout Mountain' - Grant Tarbard

'Subsistence' - C.J. Heyworth

'USA' - William Harfosh

'Tree of Life' - Neil Ellman

'Three Kinds of Failure' - Chris Hamilton Emery

'The Dillinger Brides' - Grant Tarbard

'The Ghost Self' - Jonathan Beale

'Unwritten Postcard from Oz' - Ben Fisher

'Shower in Sunshine, North Wales' - Ira Lightman

'The Gypsy Principle' - Andrew F. Giles

'stones' - Mark Paleologo

'.marks the spot' - Jonathan Beale

'September 29th 2012: For Michaelmas' - C.J. Heyworth

'The Diagnosis' Rob A. Mackenzie

'Paradise' - Dean Faulwell

'Queue the Pits' - Ira Lightman

'Darkness' - Darrell Croan

'Only' - Allison Grayhurst

'Odyssey' - Mike Cluff

'Last night' - Richie McCaffery

'white blush sob story' - Grant Tarbard

'black stamp' - Sarah Farrant

'Justice' - Klaus J. Gerken

'Galloping Consumer' - Sue Bradford

'Eleventh Hour' - Joan McNerney

'Ode to the Rejected' - Grant Tarbard

'Dirge to a Dying Black Cat' - Sy Roth

'Kwanzaa Christmas Tango' - Joe Green

'Man!' - Ira Lightman

'deep dreaming' - Sarah Farrant

'Beware' - Joan McNerney

'Dearest Eva' - Jnana Hodson

'Bowspirit' - Barry Niditch

'Blue Room' - Ben Fisher

'A Paradise Garden' - George Szirtes

The Sea Cave (Articles & Reviews)-

'Walking to Work' - C.J. Heyworth

Bios

The Screech Owl © Resurgant Press (2014)

All artwork © Annette Haines, except the portrait of John Masefield which is by Jerome Blum (1918)

The pentagram used is that which Stanislas de Guaita first published in La Clef de la Magie Noire in 1897. It is the first known appearance of the pentagram and goat-head combination and is the primary influence on the Baphomet Pentagram, the official symbol of the modern Church of Satan.

All work is the sole property of the author.

The Apple Tree
(Poetry & Prose)

Sleep

Today the sea was smiling
In a million waves,
Tonight I slumber
Wrapped in folds of love
I fall to valleys
And gravity buries me
'Neath the dirt of sleep

Spreading thorns above
Choke the autumn sun
The hero tugs at rein;
His passing coach is gone

Unveiled, the misty maiden
Diffused by night sublime
Her reflection scattered
Like endless floating petals
Thrown to flutter
And to tremble
On sleeping-shifting water

Blessed Poseidon
Waits in silence
As her carriage rolls
He knows at dawn
Disciples wake

To slash thick growth
Of soiled dreams
Resurgent bones
Arise like blades
They slay nocturnal tangle
And aching eyes do crease
Against the morning, blind

As once obscured
By pricking bramble
Is now sighted
The restored horizon.

By Martin Slidel

Folly

I have dipped my finger in the fountain
and held it to the wind.
I have slid the ladder of Lilith,
dog-deep in her cavern -
to divine and decipher the smog.

I have ascended the mountain,
swung my intuition around like a staff,
finding paradise in a pool of blood
and hell in my burning cloak.

I have numbered the quills
on a porcupine's back
and spilled the left-overs
of a left-handed bat.

Now let us cast runes in the monastery ruins
and sip moonlight through a crystal.
And I shall tell you
when the end will come.

By David Seddon

Große Geister (Large Ghosts)

(after the installation sculpture by
Thomas Schütte)

These figures could be gods
our own creations
embarrassed by their own;

or, alien visitors dancing
the Charleston
out of date and out of tune;

or, cartoon characters
with the same clothes everyday
and exaggerated smiles;

or, mimes in a Berlin park
pushing against the wind
and reality.

They could be ghosts, of course,
but can be seen only
as what we take them for

more like ourselves
than we could ever know
as puerile as our pride.

By Neil Ellman

Vampyre

For Max Schreck

Recalling the glaze of sunset yellows past
Smeared in senile brushstrokes across an open range sky,
dusk in uniform.
I feel I have lost little to the night, these people that pass are relics of my former self
I feel I am whole without the eye of light present in all its ugly clarity,
a brazen hussy for the caress of gluttony
in crescendo
No melody discernible from this rotten bow
scraping the rusted string.
I feel I can breathe in the moon night
I feel I can avoid the liars
in the spiced rum streets of the night
I feel there are songs to be sung
in the little black dress of the night
I feel there are drinks to be drunk
in the barrel dregs of the night
There are tongues to be sucked in the blackest lust of night's ardour
I feel the chest plate armour night
protecting the aorta
from the stake thrusts of uninvited loves
Coming as mist in the guise of yesterday and tomorrow,
I feel the harmless testimony of dark shop windows night
The milkless coffee night
The post train night rattling bridges like maracas
Singing with throaty gusto that
"True love doesn't conquer all,
it just has a long memory"
A fatalistic night,
a babe in arms night with the coos of a loved one close to ear
with the crack of crab shell night a long memory,
distant broken branch mistaken for a fellow in this ill forgotten snow.

By Grant Tarbard

Caff

I felt uncomfortable in the caff today,
like I'd put on 2 lbs.
I tried to lose them by thinking about it, then ordered
another coffee and poppy-seeded bagel
which came fully loaded like the gun that'll
eventually put my teeth in
and leave me with the dead eyes.
I put down the mug and watched a drop that didn't make my tongue,
trickle and die before reaching the table.

I did it again.
same.

One of the blondes leaned across,
to take my sugar pot.
"don't mind do ya hun?"   'Yes, I do.'
I said. 'May need it.'
"may need it?"   'Yep.'

"Listen Shirley,
Everyday you've been coming in here,
with your books and your pen and your
imagination and your
tattoos.
Ordering the same thing. And leaving
when the sun comes back around."

'And ?'

"And I've been serving you for
months." she said.
'and?'

"And you never take sugar in your coffee."

'I know.'
I said,
'I like to have options.'

By Ben Fisher

Anais, Anais

"talking a broken dream, with spaces, reversals, retractions, and galloping fantasies" - Anais Nin

i found you Anais Nin,
i found you and i refuse to let you go.

i feel your hot breath on my cheek.
i feel the blood moving thru your heart as

i caress and palm your breast.
i dreamt about you last night--

i noticed you out of the corner of my eye,
i stared at you, i made you blush,

i moved into your soulful space.
i long to use words to make your heart race.

i know what you are thinking, what you are not thinking,
i can see you think too hard, as well.

i want to turn my back on you, let you move behind me,
i want -- oh, Anais, Anais -- i want to let you find me too.

By Sarah Farrant

David Cameron on Scottish Independence
Tippexed speech, February 2012

there is a danger of thinking of Scotland
recruiting ground for
the future Conservative Party

I'm not here to make a case
the reason I make the case is
not just about what we. It's about who we
I am a classic case

I am proud to be
like so many others, I am proud to be
safer, not just because
our tentacles reach

we're richer, because
we're fairer. Not just because
we are saving thousands
that we and others take for granted

I also understand why people
want a Scotland where more people own
where more people keep more
where businesses can

I passionately believe
Scotland's greatest poet said
the people of Scotland
believe that
which is why I'm ready for the

By Rob A. Mackenzie

Chemistry

Topaz lives within a shop window.

Accepting the acceptance;

If only for yesterday - that:

Yesterday is done and has lived and now has been- and gone.

        This is - accepted.

The breathing chemicals

Permeate the vessels

And each corpuscle

In the psyche - pricks the skin

Among the (prickly) social conscience

Eyes lead backward away!

Stumbling ever toward the ungainable,

unliveable dream - that falsehood

The days know with all this - its-

    Fire, hell, and damnation -its safety

Keeping motivation -among the need.

Dream(s) whistle thru the grass

Ideals among the clouds. Tangible? No.

Rain falls on each shop window

    Drops of topaz of each and every (like) its form

By Jonathan Beale

Shirty Boat

two pairs dot
holes on 3mm discs
sturdify overlaps

yoked on wood
cracked to
seeping shush

shut

By Ira Lightman

Waiting for Wrecks

I did not see Alan again until
this year at the funeral of our
mutual friend. When the three
of us with others shared a house
in Hampstead (near as dammit),
he was known as Al, The Horror-
Puller, an unkind soubriquet for
one who was not driven by lust
coaxing the pretty-pretties into
bed, but most of all loved brains,
shared interests, conversations
into the wee small hours, seeking
a soulmate even then.
It had not
quite worked until he'd been married
"just the once," Al said. He'd thought he
had been too shrewd to mistake for love
mere mutual convenience:
two years only until Gill came his way,
after so amicable a sundering. "Ships
that did not pass in the night," he smiled,
too fragile to collide, but not irreparable.
"This time Parliament Hill, not Highgate,
with panorama sublime, no headstone."

By C.J. Heyworth

streets maps for lost souls
for ed costigan

eddie, i can still remember the last time
i saw you crossing the corner of spruce street
how you looked so brave then

even more courageous than when you came out
to your irish catholic parents
in the middle of a family dinner in suburban nj

at that moment
i felt guilty that talking to girls
made my hands sweat
i feel guilty that it still does
when you were the one who taught me
that it takes courage
just to be alive

to set your dreams on fire
and call it independence day

you were the one who let us know
that this dance is far from perfect

you wore your heart on your sleeve
every step of the way
like a street map for lost souls

you slept on the floors of dorm rooms
after dropping out to wait tables
in the name of love
until you could scrape up enough cash
for a shoebox of your very own
with dreams as big as mouse holes

you made flying monkeys seem beautiful
and proved that there was
no place like home

i just wish you were here now
so i could look you in the eyes
and tell you
that this dance
is far from over

By John Dorsey

Loss

I'll lose her soon I fear
My heart weeps tears of lost time
Moments gone forever in life's great battle that we all fight from birth
Etching out our existence on this turbulent world
Watching as others strive to leave their mark
Begging for more time as I watch the sands slip slowly through my fingers
Precious memories wrapped in sheets of sadness
Watching those we love return to dust
Scattered on the winds of change
Banished to reside within our hearts and memories
For all time a constant reminder of what we once had and have now lost
Leaving only emptiness and yearning for what can never be again.....

By Darrell Croan

Insomnia II

stay away morning luminescence,
you will only prolong my suffering,
and i have nowhere else to hide.

By Klaus J. Gerken
3.54am 24 August 2012

Incident on Fifty-second Street

"I sit in one of the dives
On Fifty-second Street
Uncertain and afraid."

It was Christmas Eve 1939
W.H. Auden was waiting for a sign.
"Been to China, been to Spain.
Lord, lord don't want to do it again.
The Christmas star rages with its usual vengeance.
Lord, lord give me a little transcendence."

Lord, lord that's what he prayed
At the end of a low, dishonest decade.
Drinking alone. Then who comes in?
My Uncle Joe. Auden buys him a gin.
They fall in love. There is a back room!
Boom a lay Boom a lay Boom a lay Boom!
They went back to the bar and unless I miss my dates.
Auden wrote "In Memory of W.B. Yeats."
Showed it to Joe who kept on drinking.
"I like this place" is what he was thinking.

By Joe Green

I Collect Cities, Do You?

You know how kids collect stamps?
Well, I always wanted cities -
not steaming them off the world
and bombing them flat in an album -
I just thought to go round the world
and re-arrange things a bit
so they rhyme with the country they're in.

Paris is now on The Isle of Harris -
just think of the gaiety that brings.
Lucky old Cardiff, you're on Tenerife.
Llasa has just about squeezed into Gaza

but poor Moscow fell in a watery hole
between Trinidad and Tobago.
Mexico City is not sitting pretty
and where will Tokyo go?
Is it Bonn, or Washington that will be in Gabon?

I'm afraid that I really can't say.
I thought the game was going to be fun
but it turns out completely insane.

By Philip Burton

Golden Globe

The desolation of this savage gargoyle
Who treads the framework of life
And weeps
For you choke the life in me
And leave only a silhouette.

On blue ships
In grief filled seas
These crystal tears hold such visions
That carve brutal madness
As beauty dies.

Poignancy of a sincere heart
That sees with reluctant eyes
The soulless whisper
Of a tainted race
That is ruled by blasphemy.

Shadows of the heart
Leave sough sounds in the cold night
Inaugurating the rage of angels
As the flower hangs and dies
I am the golden globe.

By Annette Haines

Yo! Sushi

Then, the diner recalls the strange delight
of the night's portal; the balsa wood limbs -
pale architects - bracket her fingers as splints
& give her structure at table, high as a kite.

What to do with her, blousy drunken sailor,
unbuilt by dinner, who clasps her implements
like knitting needles? There is a spectral bent
to the diner's face, a raw shadow - white, paler

than the rest, & she hovers over her sake, distant
as a moon. What if this sea-stage, of exotic wands
& lunar symbols, is not an uncooked demi-monde
but her raffish heart collecting signs: *I want, I hunt*

By Andrew F. Giles

The Last Man on Lookout Mountain

An avoider, they said
Dancing the roam of the phobic pack
Watch him chasse through the fingers as if they were farmer's gates,
Such a trick he scales of keeping those mercy huggers away, an arms reach priesthood
Offering up a sacrament of night time silence.

The morning dredge coughs up Thames bottom sludge
Rolling a tufty grunt up the hills of knackers yard lungs
Past worn rusk teeth and a tongue downtrodden by his peers
Those words are of little merit when uttered to the space between the dust,
Offering up a moon walk against the ice of the room vacuum.

The lights from the town shine distant
Harbour beacons to veer from toward the safety of boot black rocks
His ship shakes at the timber, rivets seduced by Delilah
A barbershop massacre witnessed by Samson and Sweeney Todd,
Offering up his locks to the caress of loneliness' temptress burlesque.

The treeless vantage of the Mount
With an eye to all that lies scattered like spilt salt across the Formica,
An escape from the orchestra pit where every instrument tunes at once
That one violin bow with no elbow room, lost in the Gotterdammerung
Of one man offering solitude as a sacrifice to immortality.

By Grant Tarbard

Subsistence

Slog as the peons did:
tussle with Mexican
fireweed strangling the
oats, having to call a halt
while more oil unclogs
the grinder, unparch throats
with swigs from the canvas
water-jug, through sweat
and grit toil each day,
each day
each day
each and every day:
forever on;
forever on.

By C.J. Heyworth

USA

Let out of your head tonight

Spanish bull rushed

They tell us its gonna be okay

Stumbling over your blinked eye

Dumb bells ring

Land of the free

Swallow up that thought

Let out of your head tonight

Stars and stripes mixed together

Picasso art

Abstract naked eyes

Let out of your eyes tonight

Home of the brave

Sitting, waiting on a park bench

For your handout

With liberty

and justice

for all

By William Harfosh

Tree of Life

(after the painting by Gustav Klimt)

Strange fruit
like diamonds
emeralds
onyx, opals
topaz-berries
hang from
the tree of life

a luxuriant sun
bathes the leaves
in citrine light

before they fall
to earth
where they
were born
and will be born
again.

By Neil Ellman

Three Kinds of Failure

1.
Between moor-charred housing, slag heaps, oaks and cenotaph,
hanging in the silly village summer, away from the clock's power
and all those ruptures to come at Forty, Fifty — it's all grey limbs now:
aging laundry, residues of meals in the cold lamb smell of the kitchen.
Is this a sort of politics above the midlife chores?
Back down from the folds of whichever night we cleaved to,
where the child's cry had reached us once, for the first time,
through several flights of heavy stairs and night swell,
though we had hardly cheated it and barely lied.

2.
Piling flowers in the damp yard when that antic wheeze
of geraniums whisks up the sill under a soulless, milk and lead skyline.
I stand there frozen, hands tight, red and white, pegging up
the mindless chronologies of the never ending, never to be, scope of me.
Windows bang through the chary town; lambs die in the ditches;
a world trickles through hedge-slurry and these winds make
shining corrugations in the new mud lane.
It's there one footprint catches your attention, narrowly cherishing
its trees and crows, reflecting what's missed and, next, what's missing.

3.
You lift and drop each photograph on the salt-stained wood
of the drawer, it's old skirts and blouses, old trams, old lipstick,
the tailored marvels that seep into this future we satisfy, truthlessly.
Everyone has detached from the stems of their smiles:
the radish cheeks, the cracking songs that made the town up once,
when cut flowers heralded no thin afternoons but ties and unities --
the itineraries of each day lined up on all the neighbours' steps
and then the bleach field taller with bunting, the dated trannies
hunting static in the lime-wash where our latest travesties poured on.

By Chris Hamilton Emery

The Dillinger Brides

Jezebel eyes the marching bands with Kohl outlines
Indistinct within the mist of gears
Turning to burn oil,
To burn the trees of paradise

She eyes with watering mouth
Saliva fading,
A look over the shoulder
Jezebel eyes the marching bands

Trumpets frozen in the early morning
"When Jewish blood flows from our knives,
all will be well"
Chalk scribbled on walls, white paint slapped across store fronts

Jezebel eyes the sudden thrust
Her hair entangles the trees and hills
Like Lilith resisting her fall,
Embracing her lust for the harried Samael

Seas, oceans, the green paintbrush smear of French fields
A grey stone church dotted here, there
Black backs of ants eyeing the picnic
Hungry with starved feelers itching for the sugars of swollen stomachs

Jezebel eyes the baggage mules
And the bed linen folded despite the haste
Suitcases tied shut with string
Loose with the speed of the nearing goggles

Jezebel eyes the Dillinger bride
A two step to remember her by
Hand in hand around the mirrored ballroom
A phone call to deceive the summer of lost luxury

Jezebel eyes the tongues lashed to pillows,
The lovers flips all fingers at ease with hips
The steam of breath, the pushing lips like riot police through the feeble front door
Breathing with the pools depth of an assassin on the ledge

Jezebel eyes the marching bands
Banners for streets that had an uneasy birth
A rite of passage for the heel against the stone
A straight lance slit of a smile viewed from the cafe distance

And studied like the aftertaste of last night's misadventure
Where the huzzahs and cheers fade when the dry mask

Of convenience's powder crumbles,
Jezebel eyes the hands wielding knives of the Dillinger brides

Walking beside the warm body they have already betrayed
In the half breed slow evening
That drapes like bordello shades over the complete unwelcoming
Tightness of the white milk moon against a slow beating chest

Jezebel eyes those half broke mules,
Scrape nails against the dirty glass of lost afternoon
Bourgeois steep gillies in gutters, Chieftains skinned like boers
The finish; China rose hibiscus wreaths before the horses of the gun carriage

By Grant Tarbard

The Ghost Self

The Ghost Self: unhyphenated; the image of the dead fish

Or just an image

Out-of-life: out-of-place

That Doppelganger that eerie double Drenched in mists

Smelling of decaying memories and Inevitable

Breath seen against iced moments

Tattoos

Beating into bleeding memories of war wounds

The soul's partial failure irritates my minds soled

The ghost self

Broken, limping across uncharted voids

Seeking undesired places

The ghost self - famished of life

Blood fading from colour to black-and-white

As dead fish on key side

Mindlessly fighting decay and flies

Once more before the final step - the last act

Left undone or unsaid- or unwritten

Distort in mirror age and memory perform a double act

To punish by deceit and gain

There was a rose garden somewhere scented and cavernous

One piercing to colour the rose red

And leave the ghost anaemic

Leaving only the ghost self - the ghost self

That Mirrored idle that never is

That once and forgot just quick

The ghost self appears big than it is

Yet from within is bigger as it consumes

By Jonathan Beale

Unwritten Postcard From Oz

Thirteen years of dirt track and creek crossings 'til we met the one bridge we couldn't cross.
And only a
hand's width apart we stood, watching it burn before our very eyes.

I've had no signal for 4 days in Herberton Australia, just a short paddle down river to the old lost town.

It would've been your Dad's birthday today.
My memories of him are alive and happy, like London in the 60s.
I won't forget my feelings, ever.
The pictures remind me of the story every time I look at them.

A minor's camp-fire feast of snags, lentils and beans by the brook.
With a viewpoint sweeter than melted chocolate, 'neath the milky way. And a hearty collection of
dreams bringing us wishes and luck.

You should see the skies, day and night.
wind, rain, shine.
I wish you were here, Francene, for one last time.
There's a meadow here that reminds me of you.

Come and meet me when I'm near. We'll be face to face, arm in arm, entangled in …..
My mind wanders sometimes.

I should turn my phone off for a little while. Haven't spent enough time by myself.
And it's raining again. In Herberton Australia.
As I'm watching the world go by like some psychedelic fashion show.

There's a full moon across the coral sea, it's dreamland.
Just wish you could see it. But your back is turned.

And it's been turned for a while.

By Ben Fisher

Shower in Sunshine, North Wales

The summer-charged local light
in the place familiar, escape from school,
the holiday let,

drops full smooth
into the porch add-on,
through the clear plastic roof,

to startle whiter the stone
jut of the cockpit window and walls.
In this boost-light, how can there be rain

passing? I don't believe it in the course
of wonder. Though I hear it percuss,
I gaze gormless as the sun pours.

By Ira Lightman

The Gypsy Principle

'Slip out of darkness, it is time.'

                    - Edwin Morgan, The Second Life

Back then as now

the hunting patterns   of nomads
& their   flickering bloodflows

suspended in rusty creeks   sssh
the air conditioning unit grows
a bass note   in its chest

The cavemen dream

           of voodoo implants
curving light years around their bodies

of the strange pseudonyms of time
& time's first love, classification

of rocky halls   & workstations
where drifters traipse loomweight dust
          over manuscripts

of the bones in their feet
             zipped under ice

        of new towns cracked
from their shells, spellbound with fright

Such funny little dreams -   the cavemen
twitch &   smile on their walkabouts
through the haunting of the   light

murmur   sotto voce

strange times to be alive, aren't they

aren't they passing?

By Andrew F. Giles

stones

a talisman laid

beside the bed

two stones

with little meaning

beyond their intention

i need you to be well

they say

in a whisper

more singular than a wind

which chooses only

one tree to play with

his closed eyes

face west

watching shadows

retrace steps

past lives

past loves

command performances

for the infidel

sight restored

they remain

wholly unlikely

yet there

resting upon everything

which was lost

which was found

faded pictures scream

let the dead

bury the dead

By Mark Paleologo

.marks the spot

'How easy it is to make a ghost'
Keith Douglas

There was blood on the street
And 'why' like an a compliment
Some beguiling set up
The police and lights and all
The scene:
A man with his eyes lightly shut
Frozen in time. Eyes blind from then on
So much noise and action
Enough to wake the dead
But not enough to wake him
Hearing on the radio
Music had seemed inappropriate
Keeping a sort of silent - vidual
For this totally strange alien moment
The curtain call, unplanned
Whose fate was a passing?
Experience for those whose eyes
Never to be forgotten
The pad seemed womblike
And the cigarette: held a meaning
A life faded into the atmosphere
How is

By Jonathan Beale

September 29th 2012: For Michaelmas

Today for Michaelmas
here I write on paper
my distant ancestors
would have pulped
to block the window
entrances for wayzgoose,
our pre-glass protection
against the coming of
dark Winter's cold.

Today we quit harvesting
blackberries that pricked
fallen Satan's rump,
defenestrated from windows
of Heaven by archangel's throw.

By C.J. Heyworth

The Diagnosis

Beyond the dolmuş rank and the harbour touts,
on the dust road marked only by snoring dogs,
the off-key muezzin murdered the early evening
call to prayer and we explained your diagnosis:

> autistic people struggle to read body language
> and social cues, to keep friends, to scent a lie,
> but often demonstrate original thinking of a kind
> seldom encountered in the neurotypical world...

A stork flapped from the hills like an apologetic myth.
"Look at the bird!" someone shouted. "A stork,"
you whispered. "I know this because I'm autistic."
You distrust protean states, deal exclusively

in specifics, and on cue the muezzin gasped his last
blast of fantastical holiness and dogs rose to laud
a miracle cat resurrected from a raging wheel.
Let sleeping dogs lie? We have awoken in you

the merciful descent of silence from the minaret,
a slant of good news; only days later, questions
and tears. You snorkel the empty pool like a bird
mapping the sky of a land without landmarks.

By Rob A. Mackenzie

Paradise

An orchid of smoke
rises from the
part of paradise
near the zoo.

No one who
notices cares.
No on who
cares notices.

These are the
new rules in
paradise, where
everything delights

in looking straight
at itself.

By Dean Faulwell

Queue the Pits

My love with the longing that
under every pestilent mile
of air away you'd bury

my weak cells to integrate
us through the planet, I'll
cough where you dig me

from where my putsch was through,
I knelt at the grass
to unlid and let me sever.

Now I see it was to you
I couldn't nor can I pass
until the world as such isn't for ever.

By Ira Lightman

Darkness

That small clear voice vibrating my inner ear, intoxicating, invigorating, it paints my soul with the blackest of night trying to wrestle that last pure innocence from my being and turn this vessel into that which I detest. Like a virus it travels along the channels of my core seeping into every pore and devouring the light that once shone so bright but now twinkles like a dying star desperate to etch out it's last ember before it is extinguished forever and replaced with something dark, something foreign, something not me...

By Darrell Croan

Only

What speaks of tenderness in the dead-blue
aftermath of human-induced horror?
When husband and wife are at odds,
seeing only the diseased boil of slaughter
then non-existence, when the pregnant woman
finds no seat nor shelter in the midst of a
crowded day?
What speaks of holding on when the world is pale
with grief and parents mock their children's love
with coldness and condescension?
What eye can see divine magnificence before
its doom? Or find greatness in what
society has ignored or condemned?

On the rafters a single flower is born.
That single flower I look to, like spending
the afternoon with the ones who have endeared,
like the pulse and thud of my infant within
or a brief morning solitude -
      open for interpretation.

By Allison Grayhurst

Odyssey

The trail does not drip
nor holds any treasure
excepting the enduring
of a daily corkscrew
which penetrates a surface
of ersatz waistcoats
and polemics;
drilling downward into
the real pith and sauciness
I plan to carry
as far as need be
to reach Ithaca again
wherever it may really be
and whenever it will
let me back in
finally.

By Mike Cluff

Last night

Last night in my dreams
people in a flea market
tried to sell me things.

It worries me that I'm
a consumer also in dreams,
not for yachts or fast cars

but jumble and junk –
old coins and medals
I didn't fight or die for.

Asleep I hoard this stuff
while you say you often
dream of losing loved ones.

By Richie McCaffery

white blush sob story

(I)

with whispers carefully,
with whispers and rumors,
with whispers of Wednesday afternoon kisses
with murmurs of passion
kept safe, kept secret.
with the blue blush of morning
swept across her cheeks rich scarlet,
sacrifice offered as sunrise dare not speak.

(II)

sacrifice served
stone at window
egg cracked slowly
alarm bells distant

beige walls, grey hands
an underline sense of menace

bags packed, white dawn
the last blush before she's gone

black stamp

after the settlement made official -- with a splodgey
black stamp, on a neatly creased piece of letter-sized paper,
a final, dignified and oddly drama less full stop.

cast into a shock of silence, not knowing what emotion to express,
I chose nothing. just a large exhalation, a relaxation,
then a determination to file and move on.

but I have been stamped. my heart still carries this black ink,
which -- as certain as my degree– is a permanent hue,
it can never be truly erased and lost in history.

Imprinted with attics of halloween bunnies, still life with woodpecker,
the tipsy tuesdays bringing a apprehensive smell of
misunderstood microbrew laced with a lungful of forgetting.

a fountain of faces follow me, they haunt me in their unresolved
absence. all those people who (it turns out) I never really knew.
their lasting black mark seems a largely mutual fakeness.

my thoughts cannot forget the pent-up misery and
wandering loneliness, of sitting cold in a room playing mendelssohn
to an empty futon; of silent tears emptying out to strangers.

posing curiously to examine this sticky blackness branding me,
I suddenly comprehend that for this printing
I wouldn't have it any other way -- I wouldn't want it to.

By Sarah Farrant

Justice
15 October 2012

Wilhelmina shot Jason
Because he didn't like
The show she was watching
On TV

The cops arrested Wilhelmina
On a misdemeanor
And let her watch the show
In jail.

When the judge
Let her out
He said:

I like the show
You were watching.
5 dollar fine.

By Klaus J. Gerken

Galloping Consumer

All sorts shuffle past,
Oh yes, those workers, observant,
"Come inside"
High heels, far too big,
While flats are the best option,
Clothes, the choice is endless!

Let's fill our stomachs
On food of the heart,
Clogging while chewing,
The sepia curtain obscures.
We shall absorb into that
Chicken feed of righteousness.

That ride of glory
To the galleries above,
Where the humble units reside.
Designers, top, middle & bottom,
It's a curse,
But not rationed.

By Sue Bradford

Eleventh Hour

Wrapped in darkness we can
no longer fool ourselves.
Our smiling masks float away.
We snake here, there
from one side to another.
How many times do we rip off
blankets only to claw more on?

Listening to *zzzzzz* of traffic,
mumble of freight trains, fog horns.
Listening to wheezing,
feeling muscles throb.
How can we find comfort?

Say same word over and over
again again falling falling to sleep.
I will stop measuring what was lost.
I will become brave.

Let slumber come covering me.
Let my mouth droop, fingers tingle.
Wishing something cool…soft…sweet.
Now I will curl like a fetus
gathering warmth into myself
hoping to awake new born.

By Joan McNerney

Ode to the Rejected

Adam carried out the deed
Under the heavy hand of the Sun
Upon the rock of his spilt seed
So he and his God could be one

The Temptress, knower of lost alphabets
In sucking mire does she dwell
In the dankest sea caves she makes the beds
For the babes of sinning fathers bound for Hell

Her lunar soul diminished, the daughter of dirt spat at as foul
Her cloak of midnight succubus, animus
Strangling the lured men-dogs of this town
Listen to the moonlight whispering — her bitterness will never pale

By Grant Tarbard

Dirge to a Dying Black Cat

hate and love sit side-by-side,
hand-in-hand in simultaneity,
at war, vexing themselves.

mired in morbid desire,
it mutilates heart-places
ringing in a pandemonium of abandonment.
innocence-emblazoned phantasms
Hiroshimize the walls.

Sagacious, purring witches
dip-stick into dreams--
a cauldron's brew
uncovering gossamer conflicts
packed in the dry-ice of anguish.

perverse confessions that follow--
black cat extricated--
are frightened children
in search of spectors,
entombed spirits,
victims of a lilting threnody.

a capricious song,
opiate of desire,
gnaws like a rat through a wall
dressed in gloomy grieving vestments
to the melancholic whining
for a lost master.

silently they muster
glaring eyes
and shuffle their shoulders
in opposite directions
humming a dirge.

By Sy Roth

Kwanzaa Christmas Tango

If you're rich, then everything's easy
You just take a jaunt to Belize
And sit on the beach and dare eat that peach
And you hardly ever feel queasy.
If you're poor, you ain't in no trouble
If there is a stock market bubble
You fell quite rested with nothin' invested
And when it breaks you get nothin' in double.
But what can you do if you is a Christmas tree Jew
And it's the third night of Kwanzaa
And you're black and Catholic and Argentinean too?
You just sing like Mario Lanza
"O Solo mio
I love Dolores Del Rio
But my sheikhy dashiki's on fire
And Bacall was so hot
In "To Have and Have Not"
And if you say not you're a liar."
And you is alone as you is writin' this poem
Alas for the Jeunesse Doree
You is alone. Alone in your home
And there's only one thing you can say:
"O Solo mio
I love Dolores Del Rio
But my sheikhy dashiki's on fire
And Bacall was so hot
In "To Have and Have Not"
And if you say not you're a liar."

By Joe Green

Man!

Casanova Casasuper
nova, foreskin forks
on fallen lightning, slugg
ish. So perhaps we talk
without X Factor helium
or understanding a good
boy may show his mother,

with teeth
it whistles through like
guitar lead drains
the bloody
lake. Space notes undergarment.

By Ira Lightman

deep dreaming

Chords breaking on discord
(sergei recites) down as I glide down

Finding myself
diving down
deep
deep
down
into the wreck
(like rich did)

I saw you-- with her --
Down at the very bottom

Paralyzed
(did you want it to be like that?)

Staring at her
Whilst she

stared back at me
With such hostile negativity
That I was scared, and also somewhat ashamed

To be watching.

I turned to head back
Just as the cleansing came

I swam up fast,
broke surface

Then remembered I had now lost you.

By Sarah Farrant

Beware

If you touch Medusa
her serpents will wrap
themselves around you.
She soars through water
with giant wings gold fins.
Hundreds of snakes
crawling from her head.

Some long to be near
Medusa to hear her hissing
lisping songs all forgetful.
She can suck blood from
throats coiling minds
past infinity before
they breathe again.

By Joan McNerney

Dearest Eva

the home trip was shorter than any desire worth pursuit followed by a week strip-mined between Wheeling and Zanesville where the alphabet winds down and begins again in Ashland or Barnesville, maybe in another language still here I'm settling down as a monk in my scriptorium or as a bootlegger distilling silos of citations and trophies or as a bachelor milking his own antiquity to that point where you no longer know if you're any good or not, you're just pushing what you have to your best abilities . not everyone comes back

By Jnana Hodson

Bowsprit

A vessel sails
on warm windy nights
along the white Cape
navigating our voyage
in the unclouded dusk
annulling our deep voices
under a full moon
of cabin fever
in subterranean smoke
and cautious shadows
over whispers of transport
keeping watch
on islands of observation
from dark glasses
our heads patted with oil
of past silhouetted love
which fishermen carry
on their open sore bodies
far from drowning memory
on the deck
filled with pitchers of wine
splattered by fingers
playing wild cards
and dice for a bed and bath
you wear a Greek cap
from a cunning runaway
with long unruly hair
wanting to be a sailor
orphaned and lost at sea
near the portholes
of your home harbor
bribing you to pick him up
with a scribbled passport
ink wise out of fear
but not his own
stolen in the darkness
from a beachcomber
without a right eye
unashamed of time
eager for
disjointed conversation
naked laughter
or smothered cupidity
in the inimical dark waters.

By Barry Niditch

Blue Room

Starting to feel the burn of
previous long days and less
long nights

The bigger the room the more
uncomfortable I feel
it's harder to switch off

They all come out at night
singers,
party goers,
hell raisers

night people

Tonight it's footsteps down the
halls
creaking up the stairs, ghosts
in the walls

ghosts with character and
substance

Their presence is rife

By Ben Fisher

A Paradise Garden

1.
And so I had to find them: fish and birds
among the strands of living lineations
in which the world was elegantly tangled.
It was all I could do with my limited store of words.
The ropes we weave are the ropes by which we're strangled.
The lines we draw are the ones that snap our patience.

It was arrow and shower homing in on me
swooping like gulls over the breaking waves,
that landscape of pure water running loose.
I wish I were as straight as a young tree.
I wish I were as taut as that light noose.
I wish it were neat pins that marked our graves.

2.
See, here those perfect circles of pure light
define a space within the mind. See, there
those arcs of grey a steady hand may hold
to a true rhythm, how they pitch, take flight,
and dip again. It's as if world could fold
in on itself and leave a gap in air.

We learn by moving. So the hand that weaves
the curious pattern where a dancer moves.
We stream in on the rhythms of the blood
as it circulates. We tremble like the leaves
in terror when the steep wind is in flood.
We're what we feel and what our logic proves.

3.
Deeper within the folds of our inner skin,
those guttural and labial caverns crushed
into viscera, we find new creatures lost
to the outer world: the curious pangolin,
the eccentric hummingbird, all the crossed
breeds of the imagination, brushed

and smeared across a hard wall in the dark.
It's where we live. Lit by the lightning jags
of neural weather we stumble as best we can
over terrain where reason leaves a mark
by which we identify the place as human
complete with its trail of bones and flints and rags.

By George Szirtes

The Sea Cave (Articles & Reviews)

Walking to Work

Going to live and work in London in my early twenties in the late 1960s was for me a very big deal, and I intended to make the most of it. It was fortunate that a group of friends from my teens were sharing a house at the crest of Crediton Hill, sandwiched between Finchley Road and West End Lane, and not far from Hampstead Heath. We said "West Hampstead", but knew that really it was Kilburn. It would have been quite straightforward to travel by Tube to just round the corner from the Old Bailey offices where I was to work, but for my first day I decided I would hop off the Tube at Trafalgar Square, and head straight down The Strand towards St. Paul's Cathedral - having grown up in a seaside resort, I just had to research how a broad thoroughfare in the heart of the capital deserved the title "strand" as that was surely was the name of the sands between the sea-wall and the tideline, wasn't it? What Londoners have always done is both use the River Thames for trading purposes, but also corralled it by building heftier and heftier defences - the line of The Strand was indeed the shoreline in earlier times, but it was the work of engineers such as Bazalgette whose navvies constructed The Victoria Embankment to hold back the Thames. Its construction had re-aligned The Strand somewhat further inland, and changed its earlier nature as domestic accommodation. One of the poets we had been encouraged to read at junior and senior school as well as university was John Masefield, and as I set off from Trafalgar Square back in the Spring of 1969 lines of his stuck with me from his poem "On Growing Older":

On Growing Older

Be with me, Beauty, for the fire is dying;

My dog and I are old, too old for roving.

Man, whose young passion sets the spindrift flying,

Is soon too lame to march, too cold for loving.

I take the book and gather to the fire,

Turning old yellow leaves; minute by minute

The clock ticks to my heart. A withered wire,

Moves a thin ghost of music in the spinet.

I cannot sail your seas, I cannot wander

Your cornland, nor your hill-land, nor your valleys

Ever again, nor share the battle yonder

Where the young knight the broken squadron rallies.

Only stay quiet while my mind remembers

The beauty of fire from the beauty of embers.

Beauty, have pity! for the strong have power,

The rich their wealth, the beautiful their grace,

Summer of man its sunlight and its flower.

Spring-time of man, all April in a face.

Only, as in the jostling in the Strand,

Where the mob thrusts, or loiters, or is loud,

The beggar with the saucer in his hand

Asks only a penny from the passing crowd,

So, from this glittering world with all its fashion,

Its fire, and play of men, its stir, its march,

Let me have wisdom, Beauty, wisdom and passion,

Bread to the soul, rain when the Summers parch.

Give me but these, and though the darkness close

Even the night will blossom as the rose.

John Masefield (who was Poet Laureate 1930 - 1967).

The Strand that Masefield had depicted, "this glittering world with all its fashion" is the one I imagined I should find, but I was fooling myself. To find what I was looking for I should have had to hire The Tardis and return to the 19th century when much of the Strand was rebuilt and the houses to the south no longer backed onto the Thames, but were separated from the river by the Victoria Embankment constructed 1865-70. This moved the river some 50 metres (164.0 ft) further away. With this change The Strand became a newly fashionable address, and many avant-garde writers and thinkers gathered here, among them Thomas Carlyle, Charles Dickens, William Makepeace Thackeray, John Stuart Mill, Herbert Spencer, and the scientist Thomas Henry Huxley. 142 Strand was the home of radical publisher and physician John Chapman, who not only published many of his contemporaries from this house during the 1850s, but also edited the Westminster Review for 42 years. The American poet Ralph Waldo Emerson was also a house guest. A different grade of publishing was promoted at the east end of Strand where Holywell Street was the hub of Victorian pornography trade, until the street was physically eliminated by the Strand road-widening in 1900. Virginia Woolf also writes about Strand in several of her essays, including "Street Haunting: A London Adventure", and T.S. Eliot alludes to The Strand in his 1905 poem "At Graduation" and in his 1922 poem "The Waste Land" (part III, The Fire Sermon, v. Page 3 258: "and along the Strand, up Queen Victoria Street").

[Thanks to Wikipedia for some research material. My recall of detail is gradually deserting me.]

It was the ghosts of all of these I was seeking as John Masefield refers to a "jostling in the Strand" in his poem "On Growing Old" which I have quoted in full. The only sureness we have is that places will change.

Yes, I did eventually reach my goal, the Reader's Digest offices next door to the Old Bailey Criminal Courts, and I'll leave for another article watching half a day of the trial of the Kray Twins – trials really are free theatre if you can bear to hang around in the queue and can spare the time.

I shall return (as General MacArthur is reported to have said when fleeing the Japanese onslaught in the Pacific in the early 1940s).

By Christopher James Heyworth

Author Bios:

Christopher James Heyworth

C J Heyworth (Christo James) is a retired college lecturer and schoolmaster from Blackpool Lancashire UK.
His poems have been published in many magazines and online, and a chapbook After Singapore & Other Poems was published by DIAL 174 Press in 2003.

George Szirtes

George Szirtes was born in Budapest in 1948 and came to England as a refugee in 1956. He was brought up in London and studied Fine Art in London and Leeds. His poems began appearing in national magazines in 1973 and his first book, The Slant Door, was published in 1979. It won the Faber Memorial prize the following year. By this time he was married with two children. After the publication of his second book, November and May, 1982, he was invited to become a Fellow of the Royal Society of Literature. Since then he has published several books and won various other prizes including the T S Eliot Prize for Reel in 2005. Having returned to his birthplace, Budapest, for the first time in 1984, he has also worked extensively as a translator of poems, novels, plays and essays and has won various prizes and awards in this sphere. His own work has been translated into numerous languages.
Beside his work in poetry and translation he has written Exercise of Power, a study of the artist Ana Maria Pacheco, and, together with Penelope Lively, edited New Writing 10 published by Picador in 2001.
George lives near Norwich with his wife, the painter Clarissa Upchurch.

Barry Niditch

B.Z. Niditch is a poet, playwright, fiction writer and teacher.
His work is widely published in journals and magazines throughout the world, including: Columbia: A Magazine of Poetry and Art; The Literary Review; Denver Quarterly; Hawaii Review; Le Guepard (France); Kadmos (France); Prism International; Jejune (Czech Republic); Leopold Bloom (Budapest); Antioch Review; and Prairie Schooner, among others.
He lives in Brookline, Massachusetts.

Jnana Hodson

Jnana celebrates observing whales and seals. He blogs at Jnana's Red Barn (jnanahodson.net).

Sarah Farrant

Sarah grew up in Sheffield, in Northern England. Since that time, she has lived in four countries, travelled on four continents and wishes to continue this tradition. She currently lives in South London with her partner Chris.

She studied English Literature and Language at the University of Leeds, graduating with First Class Honours in 2007. She had the good fortune to deeply pursue an understanding of Postcolonial literature and contemporary poetry. She wrote her undergraduate thesis on the poetics of Derek Walcott, a prolific poet from St Lucia in the Caribbean and a Nobel Prize winner.

Her poetry aesthetic is constantly evolving alongside her reading, but she would consider both the imagists and minimalists as important influences, and that feminism and left-wing politics feature deeply in her work. Whilst living in San Francisco CA, she featured on the Spoken Word scene. She has been published and her concrete poetry displayed in various places, most notably with her mini-book, Orange, published by Sac Free Press in their Poems For All series.

Ira Lightman

Ira Lightman makes public art in the North East (the Spennymoor Letters, the Prudhoe Glade, the Gatesheads) and lately Willenhall and Southampton. He devises visual poetry forms and then asks local communities to supply words that will bring them alive. He is a regular on BBC Radio 3's The Verb, celebrating Bob Dylan as poet by singing extracts and accompanying himself on the ukulele, or the anniversary of John Milton by writing iambic pentameter blindfold for a week. His books are Duetcetera (Shearsman, 2008) and Mustard Tart as Lemon and a whole raft of out of print chapbooks.

Sy Roth

He is a retired school administrator from Mount Sinai, New York and has finally found the sounds of silence and the time to think whole thoughts. This has led him to find words and the ability to shape them. He has published in Visceral Uterus, Amulet, BlogNostics, Every Day Poets, Barefoot Review, Haggard and Halloo, Misfits Miscellany, Mad Swirl, Larks Fiction Magazine, Danse Macabre, Bitchin' Kitch, Bong is Bard, Humber Pie, Poetry Super Highway, Penwood Review, Masque Publications, Foliate Oak, Miller's Pond Poetry, Pyrokinection, The Artistic Muse, Word Riot, Samizdat Literary Journal, Right Hand Pointing and The Eloquent Atheist.

Grant Tarbard

Grant worked mainly as a computer games journalist before quitting in a blaze of glory to concentrate on writing poetry, his epiphany coming after a chance encounter with Allen Ginsberg on 4am TV. His work can be seen in such magazines as The Rialto , Poetry Cornwall and Decanto. He is the creator and editor of The Screech Owl.

Joan McNerney

Joan McNerney's poetry has been included in numerous literary magazines such as Seven Circle Press, Dinner with the Muse, Blueline, 63 channels, Spectrum, and three Bright Spring Press Anthologies. She has been nominated three times for Best of the Net. Four of her books have been published by fine small literary presses.

Sue Bradford

Sue Bradford is originally from Romford in Essex. She studied English literature & language, discovering a love for Shakespeare and Chaucer while taking her A-levels. She is influenced by the works of Maya Angelou & Truman Capote. Her submission of her work has been prompted by others and the ambition to let her work been seen and critically scanned.

Klaus J. Gerken

Klaus J. Gerken was born in Cuxhaven, Germany in 1949 and lives in Ottawa, Canada. He is a poet, artist and photographer, and is the founder and editor of Ygdrasil, a Journal of the Poetic Arts, the first literary journal ever to be published on the Internet.

Richie McCaffery

Richie McCaffery lives in Pittenweem, Fife in Scotland and is a Carnegie scholar at Glasgow University in the Scottish Literature department. His first collection is 'Spinning Plates' from HappenStance Press, and he has another pamphlet collection coming early next year. His work has been accepted by The Rialto, Stand, Agenda and The Dark Horse, amongst other journals.

Michael Cluff

Mike Cluff is a full-time English, Critical Thinking and Creative Writing professor at Norco (Community) College in Southern California. he is currently putting the final touches on his tenth poetry book called The Initial Napoleon.

Allison Grayhurst

Some of the recent places where Allison's work has appeared or will soon appear include: Parabola, poetrymagazine.com; Fogged Clarity, Out of Our, Quantum Poetry Magazine, Decanto, Indigo Rising and Message in a Bottle Poetry Magazine.
Allison lives in Toronto with her husband, two children, two cats, and a dog.

Dean Faulwell

Dean Faulwell is one of the founding editors of Oink. Has published poetry and fiction in The American Poetry Review, Chelsea, On Barcelona, The Paris Review, Poetry Now, et al. Two volumes of poetry, The Distance Between Here And Now and Leaving The Atocha Station On Foot.

Rob A. Mackenzie

Rob A. Mackenzie is from Glasgow and lives in Edinburgh. His collections include 'The Opposite of Cabbage' (Salt 2009) and a pamphlet, 'Fleck and the Bank' (Salt 2012). He is reviews editor for Magma Poetry magazine.

Mark Paleologo

Mark Paleologo is an American writer, musician, and recording artist born and raised in the greater New York metropolitan area. A son of Newark, New Jersey, he now calls Boonton home. His writing reflects the serenity in the daily horrors of suburban life.

Andrew F. Giles

Andrew F Giles has work in Ambit, Magma, Equinox, Poetry Scotland, Ink Sweat & Tears, And Other Poems etc, has written on poetry for The Spectator & edits Scotland's online literary arts & culture journal New Linear Perspectives. He was recently included in the SPL's Best Scottish Poetry anthology 2011, edited by Roddy Lumsden. His article John Burnside's Poetics of Failure: a Havoc of Signs recently appeared in US journal JERRY.

Ben Fisher

Ben was a band brat from birth, crawling on the hallowed floor of Abbey Road's Studio One as his Dad worked a session.
Ben grew up to be a published writer with a plethora of experience in the music industry as a songwriter and session musician himself for many acts across the UK, Europe, the United States and Canada.
His inspiration for writing poetry was both his discovery of the work of Charles Bukowski and his friendship with the poet Grant Tarbard.
He works sporadically out of his cat's home in Laindon, Essex.

Jonathan Beale

Jonathan is from Middx England, influenced by the works of Auden, MacNeice, Catullus, Shelley, Browning, Peter Porter, George Barker, and John Health Stubbs, Paz, and Pound to name a few. He writes about music, art, architecture, nature, science, cities, and people, this is what really drives him to write. He works in mental health in south west London as he has done for ten years. Jonathan won his first prize at school in 1976 and received a picture by John Piper. He has been published in Decanto (a regular contributor for the last two years), Voices of Israel in English, Penwood Review, and MiracleEzine. He has been writing poetry practically all his life in some shape or form, or another.

Chris Hamilton Emery

Chris Emery is primarily a poet, but he also works in design and publishing. Chris is involved with a couple of small businesses and co-owns the independent publishing house, Salt, and he is joint owner of a design business, The Cover Factory, based in Cromer, England.

Neil Ellman

Neil Ellman lives and writes in New Jersey. His poetry appears in numerous print and online journals throughout the world, as well as in nine chapbooks, the most recent of which, Double-Takes, is available as a free PDF download at Fowlpox.tk.

William Harfosh

Billy Harfosh currently lives in Chiang Mai, Thailand. He is originally from Syracuse, New York. Billy was born in Beirut, Lebanon in 1985 during the Lebanese civil war. For the last year Billy has been writing in Southeast Asia. He has been published both nationally and internationally. Billy has no children, no responsibilities and one suitcase, he hopes to keep it that way.

Annette Haines

Annette Haines is an artist and poet who works from Essex, UK. She is a published poet and cooker of world class gingerbread. Her art work can be seen, and is the inspiration for, The Screech Owl.

Philip Burton

Philip Burton was a winner of The Lancaster litfest poetry competition in 2005. Recently one of his poems appeared in The Best of Manchester Poets 2, (Puppywolf pub.). He is widely published in literary magazines including Stand, PN Review, Smiths Knoll, Assent, The London Magazine, and in anthologies for children. His collections can be purchased from >www.philipburton.net

Joe Green

Joe Green, along with his friend Tm Smith, is the author of "The Limerick Homer" the longest and funnest Limerick text in the world. Completed in six weeks this true account includes James Brown, James Joyce, Marty McFly, and Apollo at the Apollo (and much else, like Ahab playing the banjo) and transcends Homer's primitive text. When not writing epic poems (The Limerick Decline and Fall of the Roman Empire is underway, the Limerick New Testament is complete) Joe waits for additional ethereal communication from the discarnate spirit of Rin Tin Tin. Joe has transcribed a book of the noble fellow's poems and songs: "The Dark Bark." Rinty's claim to have assassinated JFK should be treated with some skepticism, however. Joe also has a book of poems: "The Diamond at the End of Time: Poems of the Loneliest Ranger." His poems have appeared in every issue of "Fulcrum," in "The Battersea Review," in "Rattapallax" and even in a Christmas Calendar (which cheered him up of a bleak midwinter). His poems have also been translated into Russian. They love Rin Tin Tin there. He is quite old (born 1948) and grew up in an awful mill town in Pennsylvania, got his ass drafted, finished college at Lincoln University, Pa. He went to Catholic schools until he was, inevitably, thrown out and, at the age of six, arriving home from school, asked his mother "Who signed me up for this?" He currently lives in St. Paul, Minnesota with his wife and two daughters and doesn't socialize with any poets there. They seem quite mad and depressed.

Darrell Croan

His wife would say that he always has an air of mysteriousness about him, of this he isn't too sure. He married Laura on the 17 May 2007 and regretted it ever since. They were made for each other and every day he is with her he thanks the universe for bringing them together. He has two gorgeous kids, is a full time Dad who writes short stories and poetry when he gets the chance.

John Dorsey

John Dorsey currently resides in Toledo, Ohio. He is the author of several collections of poetry, including harvey keitel, harvey keitel harvey keitel, with S.A. Griffin and Scott Wannberg (Butcher Shop Press/Rose of Sharon Press/Temple of Man, 2005), Teaching the Dead to Sing: The Outlaw's Prayer (Rose of Sharon Press, 2006), and Sodomy is a City in New Jersey (American Mettle Books, 2010). His work has been nominated for the Pushcart Prize.

David Seddon

David Seddon was born in Liverpool and became interested in poetry from an early age. Liverpool is a very cultural city, full of the arts and with a thriving poetry community. He has written since his teens, but life circumstances made him take a break until a year ago. Studying for his MA in counseling has rejuvenated his interest in poetry at a time when he got in touch with his deepest self. He reads poetry voraciously every day and always has about 4 books on the go at once.

Martin Slidel

Martin was born in Portsmouth, United Kingdom in 1970. He has a 2009 MA Art & Design in Education. University of LondonHe lives and works in London.

The Screech Owl © Semprini Publishing (2012) All rights belong with the authors.

www.ingramcontent.com/pod-product-compliance
Lightning Source LLC
Chambersburg PA
CBHW071326040426
42444CB00009B/2098